Treasures
from Sudan

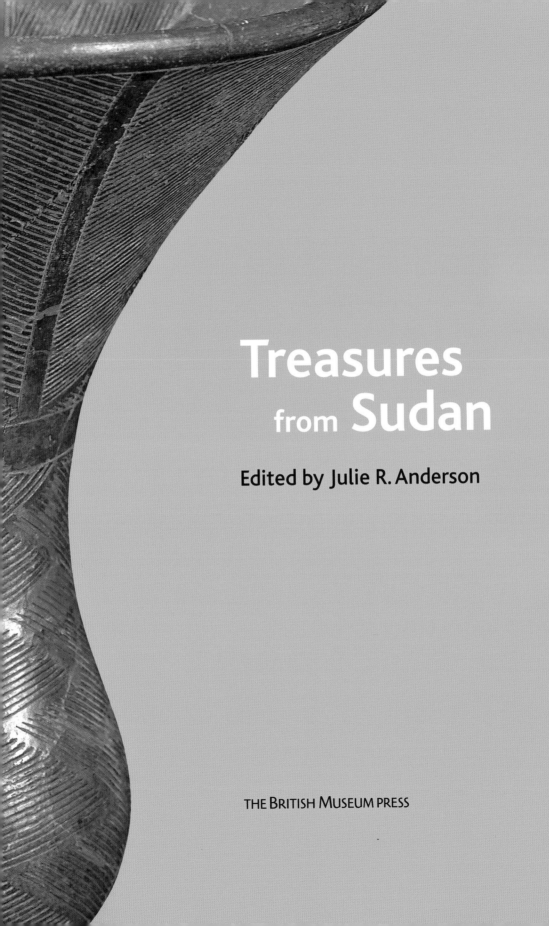

Treasures
from Sudan

Edited by Julie R. Anderson

THE BRITISH MUSEUM PRESS

First published in 2004 by

The British Museum Press

A division of The British Museum Company Ltd

46 Bloomsbury Street

London WC1B 3QQ

A catalogue record for this book is available from the British Library

ISBN 0 7141 1965 2

Designed by Harry Green

Typeset in Bliss

Printed in Spain by Grafos SA, Barcelona

Contents

Preface

This book has been written to accompany *Sudan: Ancient Treasures*, a special exhibition mounted initially at the British Museum to celebrate the centenary of the founding of Sudan's first museum in 1904, and to promote wider knowledge of the country's great archaeological heritage. A collaborative project of the British Museum and the National Corporation for Antiquities and Museums, the exhibition, drawn entirely from the collection of the Sudan National Museum in Khartoum, consists of over 300 representative objects dating from the earliest periods of attested human society in the Nile Valley through to the Islamic period. Many of the antiquities are recent archaeological discoveries. Most have never before left Sudan or been on public display.

Supplementing the larger catalogue of the exhibition, also named *Sudan: Ancient Treasures*, this smaller volume contains a brief essay on Sudan's history, followed by a choice selection of the exhibition's more important pieces together with photographs of key places and sites. Edited by an authority on Sudan's ancient and medieval past, *Treasures from Sudan* serves as a concise and accessible introduction both to the fine collection of the National Museum in Khartoum and to the history, art and archaeology of the Middle Nile Valley.

W.V. Davies
Keeper
Department of Ancient Egypt and Sudan
The British Museum

An Islamic mud-brick and stone fort, situated on top of a rocky outcrop near the Fourth Cataract of the Nile.

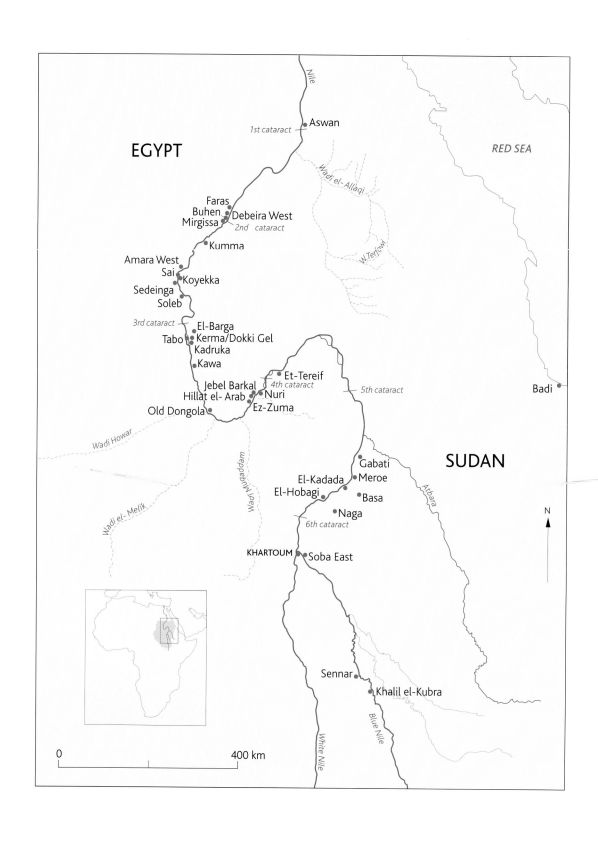

EGYPT

RED SEA

Nile

1st cataract — Aswan

Wadi el- Allaqi

Faras
Buhen
Mirgissa Debeira West
2nd cataract
Kumma

W. Terfow

Amara West
Sai
Koyekka
Sedeinga
Soleb

3rd cataract
El-Barga
Tabo Kerma/Dokki Gel
Kadruka
Kawa

Et-Tereif
4th cataract
Jebel Barkal
Hillat el- Arab Nuri
Old Dongola Ez-Zuma

5th cataract

Badi

Wadi Howar

Gabati
El-Kadada Meroe
El-Hobagi
Basa

SUDAN

Atbara

Wadi Muqaddam

Naga

Wadi el- Melik

6th cataract

KHARTOUM Soba East

N

Sennar
Khalil el-Kubra

White Nile

Blue Nile

0 400 km

UPPER EGYPT	LOWER NUBIA	UPPER NUBIA	CENTRAL SUDAN

300,000	300,000		300,000
		PALAEOLITHIC	
8500	8500	8500	
		MESOLITHIC	
5500	5500	5500	
5000	5000		5000
4500	4500	NEOLITHIC	4500
4000	4000		4000
3500	A-Group: c. 3700–2800 BC	3500	Pre-Kerma: c. fourth millennium BC–c. 2600 BC
Early Dynastic period: 3100–2686 BC			
3000		3000	
2500	?	2500 KINGDOM OF KUSH Ancient Kerma: 2500–2050 BC	2500
Old Kingdom: 2686–2181 BC			
2000 First Intermediate period: 2181–2055 BC	C-Group: 2300–1600 BC	2000 Middle Kerma: 2050–1750 BC	2000
Middle Kingdom: 2055–1650 BC *			
Second Intermediate period: 1650–1550 BC		Classic Kerma: 1750–1500 BC	
1500		1500	1500
New Kingdom: 1550–1069 BC			
1000 Third Intermediate period: 1069–747 BC		1000 KINGDOM OF KUSH	1000
500 25th Dynasty: 747–656 BC		500 Napatan phase: ninth–fourth centuries BC	500
Late period: 747–332 BC			
Ptolemaic period: 332–30 BC			
0		0 Meroitic phase: fourth century BC–fourth century AD	0
Roman period: 30 BC–AD 395			
500 Byzantine period: AD 395–640	X-Group: Ballana culture: fourth–sixth centuries AD **	500 Post-Meroitic: fourth–sixth centuries AD ***	500
Islamic period: AD 640–present	Nobadia: sixth–end of seventh centuries AD	MEDIEVAL PERIOD	Alwa: sixth century AD–1504
1000		1000 Makuria: sixth century AD–1323/1365	1000
1500	Dotawo: AD 1323–c. 1500	1500 ISLAMIC PERIOD AD 1323–present	1500
Ottoman Period: AD 1517–1917		Funj Sultanate: AD 1504/5–1820	
		Turkiya: AD 1820–81	
		Mahdiya: AD 1881–98	

* (to the Fourth Cataract) ** (First to Third Cataracts) *** (upstream of the Third Cataract)

An introduction to the history of Sudan

S udan is the largest country in Africa, covering approximately 2.5 million square kilometres, over ten times the area of the United Kingdom. For thousands of years it has been the area of contact between the peoples of Central Africa and those from the Mediterranean world. To celebrate the centenary of the founding of the first museum in Sudan, one of the oldest in Africa, the British Museum and the Sudan National Museum have jointly created a unique exhibition entitled *Sudan: Ancient Treasures*, which opens in the British Museum in 2004 and will subsequently travel to other venues both in the United Kingdom and abroad. A selection of exhibition highlights that embody Sudan's rich archaeological heritage are presented here. All come from the National Museum in Khartoum and most have never been seen outside Sudan before. Many are new discoveries made in the last few years, and are the products of ongoing archaeological research in the region. Ranging in date from about 8500 BC to the nineteenth century AD, these antiquities cover numerous different cultures and people.

The first settlers in northern Sudan date back about 300,000 years. These people are identified in the archaeological record primarily by the stone tools (lithics) they manufactured and the techniques they used. Based upon the kinds of artefacts being made, the prehistoric period is divided into three sections: the Palaeolithic (*c.* 2,500,000–9000 BC), the Mesolithic (*c.* 9000–5500/5000 BC) and the Neolithic (5000–3000 BC). Throughout these phases, the climate fluctuated between wet and dry periods which had a dramatic effect on the environment, plants and animals.

Well-preserved Palaeolithic sites are extremely rare because millennia of erosion have frequently worn away the ancient ground surfaces leaving only the lithics, usually a mixture of large handaxes and choppers. Composite tools, consisting of small flints set into wooden or bone handles, started to be produced during this period, and at Sai red and yellow iron oxides were ground into pigments and perhaps used for ritual purposes. This is one of the earliest attested uses of colour in the world. Towards the end of the Palaeolithic, pottery appears for the first time in Sudan and shortly becomes one of the most common items found on archaeological sites.

1 Sentinel lion

Basa; Kushite, mid-first century BC; SNM 24393;
H 1.72 m

This imposing lion sits on its haunches with
tail wrapped around the left side and its
mane depicted in low relief. Two cartouches,
enclosing a royal name and titles written in
Meroitic hieroglyphs, are inscribed on its
chest. They read, 'The Lord of the Two Lands,
the king ever-living Amanikhabale'. This was
one of several lions found sitting on the
edge of a man-made reservoir (*hafir*), an
invaluable water resource for nomadic
peoples and herds during the dry season.
The lion symbolized the power of the
Kushite king and would have served as a
keen reminder of the State's authority to
those forced to gather at the water source.
Also invoked here is Apedemak, the Kushite
god of war and fertility, who is often
depicted as a human with the head of a lion.

Around the eighth millennium BC, with the onset of more clement conditions, people spread across much of what is now the Sahara Desert. Mesolithic peoples sought favourable places, including the Nile Valley, where they lived along its banks and tributaries in semi-permanent settlements engaging in hunting and gathering, particularly of fish and molluscs. They used grinding stones, small flints and composite tools, as well as awls for piercing leather, and wood and bone harpoons for fishing. The dead were buried within their settlements; lip plugs (see cat. 4) have been found in several graves, indicating that the people practised body adornment.

Animal husbandry and farming began during the Neolithic, and was practised in the Eastern and Western Deserts (see cat. 7) as well as the Nile Valley. In some cases this led to a more sedentary population, the creation of settlements and large burial grounds in places like Kadruka and el-Kadada in northern Sudan. Two distinct types of graves are found at these sites. A few richly equipped tombs belonged to the social elite and included beakers, figurines and combs (see cats 5, 6, 8, 9). Occasionally the main burial was accompanied by an individual who had been sacrificed to accompany the deceased into the afterlife. Graves of poorer people were more numerous and sparsely furnished. Together they provide evidence for the beginning of social stratification, the first development

2 The Sudan National Museum

Sudan has a rich cultural heritage embodied in numerous archaeological sites and countless ancient artefacts. Inaugurated in 1971, the Sudan National Museum in Khartoum is the successor to the Khartoum Museum, the first museum in Sudan, established at Gordon Memorial College. Exhibiting artefacts from the Prehistoric era through to the early Islamic period, the National Museum houses one of the finest collections of antiquities in the world, which continues to grow as a result of an expanding programme of fieldwork and new archaeological discoveries.

towards a complex society. Agriculture offered many advantages for human development, but with it came a greater reliance on a stable and predictable climate. Increasingly dry conditions during the sixth millennium BC caused the population to move away from the deserts towards the Nile. The river became more important, ultimately becoming the longest oasis in the world.

Following the Neolithic, during the fourth millennium BC, two distinct cultures emerged. To the south of the Second Cataract of the Nile, a culture known as Pre-Kerma can be recognized in the archaeological record. The region it covered has yet to be clearly defined, and so far it is known only in a few places, notably Kerma and Sai, where many grain storage pits and traces of numerous wooden buildings have been discovered. Post-holes are the only remains of the timber buildings, animal enclosures and massive defensive palisades preserved in the archaeological record. From these it is possible to reconstruct the 4–5-metre circular huts of the Pre-Kerma people and the lines formed by the fences of the livestock stockades.

To the north, near the ancient Egyptian border in an area called Wawat by the Egyptians, a contemporary population known as the A-Group thrived. The A-Group people, situated between the First and Second Cataracts of the Nile, are characterized by their use of numerous imported Egyptian goods, settlements containing storage pits and small huts of wooden construction, distinctive 'eggshell' pottery and their burial customs. From this point onward, pottery remained one of the finest products of the northern and central Sudanese Nile Valley up to the end of the medieval period over 4,000 years later. The A-Group served as middlemen, trading Egyptian goods south and Pre-Kerma items north. The Pre-Kerma people do not appear to have traded directly with Egypt. Towards the end of the Pre-Kerma period in the third millennium BC, the contact between the A-Group and Pre-Kerma peoples appears greatly reduced and few imported Egyptian goods are found south of the Second Cataract.

Around 3000 BC, the Egyptians were drawn into the region, led by a desire for raw materials and the riches of sub-Saharan Africa. An inscription was left by an Early Dynastic king (3100–2686 BC) near the Second Cataract, and during the Old Kingdom (2686–2181 BC) a settlement was founded at Buhen. Contemporary with Egypt's Old Kingdom, a new indigenous state, which eventually became the Kingdom of Kush, developed in northern Sudan near the Third Cataract. Archaeologists named it the 'Kerma culture' (c. 2500–1500 BC), after the site of Kerma, the earliest urban centre in sub-Saharan Africa (see cat. 13) and the capital of the Kushite kingdom. Over a period of 1,000 years, Kerma grew into a highly developed town with a monumental temple and religious complex, royal palace, storehouses, administrative buildings, houses, kilns, metalworking furnaces and substantial defenses. Kerma pottery is among the finest ever produced in the Nile Valley (see cats 11, 14, 16). The kingdom's prosperity was based on agriculture, particularly in the fertile Nile basins, and on animal husbandry. The success of the latter is dramatically demonstrated by the vast number of sacrificed animals included with the royal burials; one tomb is associated with 4,000 cattle. Four kilometres to the east of the town lies the main cemetery with over 30,000 burials (see cat. 10) and several large funerary temples.

Expansion of the Kushite kingdom appears to have been rapid and it quickly gained control of the Nile Valley, from Sai Island in the north to beyond the Fourth Cataract of the Nile. Kush became Egypt's major trading partner (see cat. 12) because it controlled access to the wealth of sub-Saharan Africa. Although the Egyptians described Kush in derogatory terms such as 'wretched' or 'vile', the Egyptian Middle Kingdom pharaohs also built a series of massive fortresses along their southern border between the First and Second Cataracts and beyond. This is a clear indication of Kush's power and the threat that it posed.

Around 1700 BC, the Kingdom of Kush became the most powerful state in the Nile Valley. With the withdrawal at the end of the Middle Kingdom of the Egyptians from Nubia, the area between the First and Fourth Cataracts, the Kushites rapidly filled the power vacuum, ruling a region that extended from at least the First Cataract possibly as far upstream as the Fifth Cataract. The latest Kushite kings of the Classic Kerma period, contemporaries of the Egyptian 17th Dynasty, were extremely powerful. Their might is highlighted by their enormous burial mounds, which contained rich grave goods and, in one case, around 400 sacrificed individuals (see cat. 15). Allied with the Hyksos, who had invaded northern Egypt from Palestine, they posed a substantial threat to the small Egyptian state centred at Thebes. Caught in the middle, the beleaguered Egyptian pharaohs faced Kushite raids (see cats 19, 20).

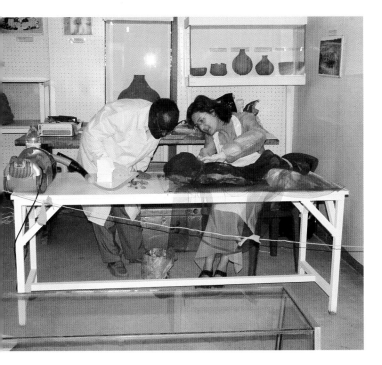

3 Conservation work at the Sudan National Museum

Conservators Hyder Hamid Mukhtar and Barbara Wills of the Sudan National Museum and British Museum, respectively, cleaning and consolidating a recently excavated natural mummy and shroud (SNM 31268) from the medieval cemetery at et-Tereif, in preparation for the exhibition *Sudan: Ancient Treasures*. In contrast with burials of an earlier date, medieval Christian graves were sparsely furnished, normally lacking grave goods. The body was wrapped in a coarsely woven brown shroud, which in this case was held in place by a cord wrapped around the head, neck, waist, knees and feet. Usually the body was laid on its back and placed in a narrow shaft orientated east–west, but this individual was either too large for the grave or had been deliberately placed in a flexed position with the knees bent.

Kush was too powerful a neighbour for the Egyptians to bear and in the early 18th Dynasty a revitalized Egypt invaded Kush. Beginning under Kamose (1555–1550 BC), Egypt and Kush engaged in a struggle for power that resulted in the conquest of the latter by Thutmose I (1504–1492 BC). Evidence from Kerma suggests that despite its massive defenses, the town was violently destroyed by the Egyptians around 1500 BC. The southern border of the Egyptian empire was established just south of Abu Hamed. Further south, the Neolithic cultures appear to have remained, while those in the west had cultural contacts with the Chad Basin. Both areas were beyond the reach of the Egyptian rulers of the Nile Valley.

In due course, Nubia was administered by a viceroy called the 'king's son of Kush', who represented the pharaoh. He was aided by Egyptianized local Nubian families (see cat. 22). They ensured a steady flow of Nubian tribute, particularly gold, to Egypt, and oversaw a monumental building programme between the First and Second Cataracts (see cats 23–5, 27) including the construction of temples, such as Sedeinga (see cat. 26), and fortified towns. From time to time punitive expeditions, such as that conducted by Pharaoh Seti I against Irem, an area probably located in the northern Butana and region south of the Fifth Cataract (see cat. 27), proved to be necessary.

As a result of internal problems, the Egyptians withdrew from Nubia during the early eleventh century BC. This left a power vacuum that gave rise to a second Kushite kingdom, based downstream of the Fourth Cataract, in the ninth century BC. These new rulers can be first identified in the royal burial ground at el-Kurru, where initially they followed local funerary customs. Rapidly, however, they adopted Egyptian religion and practices, worshipping Egyptian gods, particularly Amun, who was believed to reside in the mountain of Jebel Barkal (see cats 32, 33, 36, 37). A large religious complex developed at the mountain's foot.

In the mid-eighth century BC, the Kushite kings invaded Egypt as champions of the Egyptian state god Amun. Under Piankhi and his immediate successors, known in Egyptian history as the pharaohs of the 25th Dynasty (see cats 30, 33, 36), the Kushites ruled an empire that stretched from the borders of Palestine possibly as far upstream as the Blue and White Niles, uniting the Nile Valley from Khartoum to the Mediterranean. After ruling Egypt for almost a hundred years, in the mid-seventh century BC the Kushites were expelled by the Assyrians; however, the Kushite kingdom remained powerful, flourishing in Sudan for another thousand years (see cats 38, 40)

Jebel Barkal remained the main religious centre, while Meroe, a city further upstream, gained significance, possibly becoming the principal royal residence. The main royal burial ground was moved there in the third century BC, probably because of dynastic change. For the next six hundred years, most Kushite rulers were buried in rock-cut tombs under pyramids with funerary chapels (see cats 46–8). The Kushites maintained close contacts with Egypt. A rich combination of Pharaonic, Hellenistic and Roman influences are visible in many aspects of the culture, which also retained its indigenous African traditions. This is particularly notable in their art, religion (see cats 41, 43) and, in the language, known as Meroitic (see cat. 43), which has yet to be deciphered.

By the fourth century AD, the Kushite kingdom was in decline and fragmented. Royal burials at Meroe came to an end. Once again, the elite were buried in rich graves under large mounds, such as those at el-Hobagi, rather than pyramids. This was a return to the indigenous tomb monument present from the first Kushite kingdom of Kerma 3,000 years earlier. Many elite burials were accompanied by traditional Kushite symbols of authority, including a large array of weaponry and horse trappings (see cat. 50). These individuals were clearly holders of political power, but it is uncertain whether they were kings in their own right. Kushite culture did not disappear immediately; funerary customs and the worship of the old gods continued (see cat. 51), only to be brushed away by the arrival of Christianity in the sixth century AD.

The political situation became stable by the mid-sixth century AD and the rulers of the three medieval kingdoms, Nobadia, Makuria and Alwa, governed the Nile Valley from the First Cataract to the Blue and White Niles. Missionaries from the Byzantine Empire converted these kingdoms to Christianity and thus introduced a marked cultural change into the region (see cat. 52). Churches replaced temples (see cats 53, 54) and simple burials replaced the grand tombs of the earlier pagan rulers. With the adoption of Christianity and Islam, the view of the afterlife made the provision of grave goods unnecessary.

After a brief period of conflict with their neighbours to the north, thereby securing their borders, the medieval kingdoms flourished. The introduction of the *saqia* (waterwheel) for irrigation allowed agriculture to expand, which led to a population explosion. Villages, towns, monasteries and massive fortresses lined the banks of the River Nile. Artists attained new heights of achievement, particularly in the fields of mural art, pottery production and decoration. Fine churches were built and decorated with carved stone elements and wall paintings (see cats 52, 53). Wide-ranging trade and diplomatic contacts were established with the Muslim world (see cat. 57) and the Byzantine Empire. Goods were even imported from as far away as China.

From the twelfth century onwards, dynastic strife, poor relations with the Ayyubids and Mamelukes in Egypt, and the rise of the Funj in the south brought about the final collapse of the medieval kingdoms. By AD 1500, the country was largely Islamic, part of a gradual process that had begun in the seventh century AD. Shortly afterward, the north and Red Sea coast came under Ottoman control and central Sudan was governed by the sultans of the Funj (see cat. 58) based at Sennar on the Blue Nile. The Funj invited *'Ulama* (Islamic scholars) from abroad, as well as those from within Sudan to teach, and to establish *khalwas* (Koranic schools) and mosques. The landscape began to change as holy Islamic sheikhs were buried within *qubba*, tomb monuments reminiscent of the pyramids of the earlier Kushite period (see cat. 60).

In AD 1819–20 Mohammed Ali, the ruler of Egypt, dispatched his armies up the Nile (see cat. 59) and occupied northern and central Sudan. The Turkiya, as this period is known, was brought to an end by the nationalist movement of the Mahdi whose triumphant capture of Khartoum in January AD 1885 was to lead to Anglo-Egyptian involvement in Sudan ten years later and eventually to the birth of the modern Republic of the Sudan.

4 Lip plugs

El-Barga; Mesolithic or early Neolithic; SNM 31136; L 0.9–2.4 cm

Discovered in adult graves near the mouths of the individuals, these small dumb-bell-shaped items of jewellery were inserted through holes made in the upper or lower lips or nose. They have been carefully smoothed and are made from ivory, carnelian, amazonite and mesolite. A large proportion of such lip plugs has come from the burials of women. Though uncommon in Egypt, they have been frequently found in Sudan, dating particularly from the last thousand years BC. This type of jewellery is still worn in East Africa, and modern variations are currently popular in many countries.

5 Beaker

El-Kadada; Neolithic; SNM 26899; H 27.7 cm

Caliciform beakers have a very distinctive and unusual shape, with broad, flaring mouths, narrow necks and pendulous bases. Although they are relatively rare, they have been discovered both in central Sudan and to the north in Upper Nubia. They are made using a combination of coil technique for the upper part and hand-modelling for the base. Geometric patterns decorate the exterior and vessel mouth, and are frequently filled with white gypsum to highlight the design. These ceramic beakers have been found almost invariably in graves and it has been suggested that they were used for funerary libations.

6 Figurines

Kadruka; Neolithic; SNM 28731 and 26861; H 19.9 cm and 19.6 cm

These extremely stylized figurines, both of which were discovered in tombs, have an abstract appearance and are among the earliest sculptures of the human form from the Nile Valley. The bodies have been reduced to simple proportioned outlines accentuated by the coloured veins in the finely polished sandstone. The roll of stomach fat indicated on one figure is emphasized by such a vein. No sexual features are shown and only hints of anatomical details, such as eyes or shoulders, are given. Many Neolithic figurines from the Near East and Nile Valley have been described as female fertility symbols (see cat. 8), but as the sexual characteristics are not specifically depicted on these statues, it is difficult to assign such a meaning to them and their purpose remains uncertain.

7 Survey and excavation in the Wadi Howar

The Wadi Howar, the so-called 'Yellow Nile', is located on the southern edge of the Sahara, and was once an important tributary of the Nile. Recent desert excavations and surveys conducted there have discovered more than two thousand prehistoric sites dating between the sixth and the second millennia BC. These sites are typically covered with a dense scatter of lithics, grindstones, bones and pot sherds. After the second millennium BC the region became too arid to support a permanent population.

8 Female figurine

El-Kadada; Neolithic; SNM 26970; H 6.8 cm

Neolithic female figurines are usually stylized representations of the human body (see cat. 6). This terracotta figure, made of a series of spheres, lacks arms and legs, and the base has been flattened, perhaps to allow the statuette to stand. The breasts are prominent, while the hips are full and well-rounded, probably indicating fertility. Unusually, the navel is shown. The hair, a stylish coiffure perched on top of the small head, appears as a pecked cap. Incised lines around the neck probably represent necklaces, while those around the hips may indicate tattooing, scarification or decorated garments. In Sudan this type of figure has been found thus far only at el-Kadada.

9 Comb

Kadruka; Neolithic; SNM 26870; L 9.1+ cm

Ivory, from elephants and hippopotami, was used primarily for personal ornaments, including combs, bracelets, needles and cosmetic boxes. Ivory blocks, some midway through the carving process, have been discovered in graves. This ivory comb was probably made from a section of elephant tusk. It is highly polished and had seven teeth, although now only the bases of most remain. While common in later periods, it is unusual to find a comb dating to as early as the Neolithic. Combs may have been used for grooming or decoration: in this context, it is interesting to note the elegant hairstyles shown on some Neolithic figures (see cat. 8).

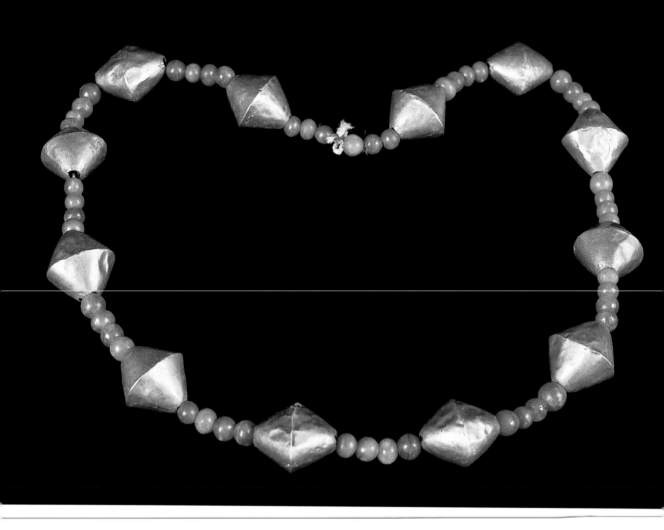

10 Necklace

Kerma; Classic Kerma; SNM 1139; gold bead:
L 3.0 cm

Most of the tombs at Kerma were
systematically plundered in antiquity,
so gold and jewellery were probably much
more common than is suggested by the
finds excavated by archaeologists. This fine
necklace of twelve lozenge-shaped gold
beads and fifty round carnelian beads was
discovered in a small basket, among the
spoils of a pilfered tomb, where it had
probably been forgotten or overlooked by
robbers. Amulets, bracelets, rings and beads
were also found there, an indication of the
tomb's original wealth.

11 Bowl

Kerma; Ancient Kerma; SNM 25107; H 11.2 cm

This hand-made red ceramic bowl with black rim is decorated in an unusual and pleasing fashion. Incised crosshatching, underlined by a groove made with a potter's comb, runs in a band around the rim. The body is covered in a series of short double lines of raised dots or bosses, and the bottom is further decorated with comb imprints. The outside of the bowl appears powdery because the red slip covering the surface was applied after the vessel was fired.

12 Mirror

Mirgissa; Classic Kerma; SNM 14043; face: L 8.5 cm

Probably an import from Egypt, this copper-alloy mirror springs from a papyrus-shaped handle, the top of which has two falcons perched in the leaves on opposite sides. The disc is almost circular and was inserted into the handle with a short tang fixed by a rivet. It would have been highly polished to reflect images. The mirror was discovered protectively wrapped in fabric in a tomb containing numerous imported items. Similar mirrors have been found in Egypt, where they served both functional and religious uses. Though rare, mirrors have been found among graves dating as early as the Ancient Kerma period.

13 Temple at Kerma

Kerma is the site of the earliest urban settlement in sub-Saharan Africa. This massive
mud-brick ruin stands almost 20 m high and forms the remains of a great temple that dominated
the town of Kerma, the capital of the Kingdom of Kush, towards the end of the first Kushite
kingdom in the Classic Kerma period. Known as the 'Western Deffufa', the latter a Nubian word
for an imposing man-made structure, it was the final product of a long series of architectural
modifications and renovations undertaken in the sacred precinct throughout the Kushite period.

14 Beaker

Kerma; Classic Kerma; SNM 5282; H 9.5 cm

The high point of hand-made ceramic production in Sudan is represented by the tulip-shaped Kerma beakers. They have extremely thin walls and highly polished, lustrous red bodies that are separated from the black-topped rims by a characteristic grey transitional stripe. The pot face was burnished with a pebble to create the polished surface, while red ochre was applied to achieve the colour. The vessel was fired in an oxygen-rich atmosphere and then tipped upside down and placed in an oxygen-poor atmosphere to create the black rim. These beakers are found over a wide area, both in tombs and in humble settlements, ranging from Kerma well into the region of the Fourth Cataract.

15 Scorpion plaque

Kerma; Classic Kerma; SNM 1036; L 6.5 cm

A scorpion, shaped in high relief, adorns this faience plaque. The hole at the top would have enabled it to be sewn on to clothing or strung on a necklace as an amulet. It was deemed worthy of repair, as four repair holes are present on either side of the scorpion's tail. This plaque and one other were found on the abdomen of an individual who had been sacrificed and buried with a Kushite ruler. It was probably thought to have protective properties and may have played a role in the religious cult. Fragments of quartz scorpion sculptures were found with those of other animals in spoil heaps that originated from another Kushite royal tomb.

16 Ostrich-shaped vessel

Kerma; Classic Kerma; SNM 1134; H 15.5 cm

This unusual ceramic vessel has been given animal traits that
suggest an ostrich, including small wings, a large bulbous body,
a long curved neck and a tail. Ostrich feathers were used in fans,
while vessels and beads were made from the eggshells, but
ostriches themselves are rarely represented in the Kerma period.
Images found in inlays, wall paintings and mica ornaments are
uncommon, though the birds were frequently depicted earlier
in prehistoric rock art of the Neolithic period. Along with
another such vessel, this specimen was found near the chapels
associated with the Kushite royal tombs.

17 Hair slides

Kerma; Ancient Kerma; SNM 25115; D 4.6–4.7 cm

Frequently found at Kerma and on other Kerma period sites,
this egg-shaped jewellery was created from bivalve shells. They
are extremely light and fragile and frequently show signs of repair.
While they were found within tombs associated with individuals,
it is difficult to determine their exact function. It has been suggested
that they were earrings or hair ornaments, although the narrowness
of the keyhole slit would make fastening them to an ear difficult.
Shell jewellery does not seem to have been worn much during the
later Classic Kerma phase and may have gone out of fashion.

18 Pendant

Kerma; Classic Kerma; SNM 31197; H 1.8 cm

Gold jewellery dating to the Kerma period
is rarely found, as few pieces appear to have
escaped ancient robbers (see cat. 10). This
egg-shaped rock crystal was placed within
two thin perpendicular bands of gold sheet
to form a pendant. The gold setting was
simply manufactured by using pressure.
Several rock crystal deposits were found
in the massive mud-brick temple at Kerma
known as the 'Western Deffufa' (see cat. 13),
and many rock crystal beads were also
discovered in the royal tombs there. This
suggests that rock crystals were valued
highly during the Classic Kerma period.

20 Vessel of Sobeknakht

Kerma; Classic Kerma/Egyptian 17th Dynasty;
SNM 1087; H 13.6 cm

Skilfully worked and polished, this decorative
travertine flask bears a funerary inscription in
Egyptian hieroglyphs identifying both its
contents and original owner: 'A gift which
[the king] gives, that he may give incense
and unguent to the spirit of the Governor,
Hereditary Prince, of Nekhen (Hierakonpolis),
Sobeknakht'. It is one of numerous Egyptian
objects found buried in the royal tombs at
Kerma. Originally, the flask would have
belonged in the tomb of the Egyptian owner
and was almost certainly plundered during
a Kushite raid into Egypt. Such attacks have
been confirmed by a 17th Dynasty
inscription recently discovered in a tomb
at Elkab, in Upper Egypt.

19 Stela with a figure of a king

Buhen; Classic Kerma/Egyptian 17th Dynasty; SNM 62/8/17; H 26 cm

A schematic figure of a striding king is carved in relief on this roughly
shaped sandstone stela. He wears the white crown of Upper Egypt,
a short skirt, and carries a mace and a longbow with three arrows.
It has been suggested, both from its find site and on artistic grounds,
that depicted here is a Kushite king wearing some of the royal symbols
of an Egyptian pharaoh. During the Classic Kerma period, the Kushites
carried out at least one major invasion of Upper Egypt (see cat. 20).
This implies that the portrayal of a Kushite king in pharaonic regalia
may have been more than just an idle aspiration on their part.

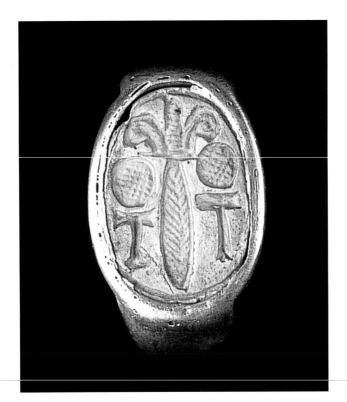

22 Stela of Amenemhat

Debeira West; New Kingdom, 18th Dynasty
(1473–1458 BC); SNM 63/4/7; H 1.07 m

Decorated with hieroglyphic inscriptions and
scenes of the tomb owner and his family,
this granite stela of the 'Chief of Teh-khet,
Amenemhat' asks the funerary gods to
provide goods and benefits for the tomb
owner's spirit in the afterlife. Although
appearing Egyptian, Amenemhat is known to
have been Nubian. He belonged to an elite
local family that was 'Egyptianized' and
governed the region of Teh-khet (Debeira
and Serra) on behalf of the Pharaonic
administration. This position was previously
held by his father, Rwia, and older brother,
Djehutyhotep. Other officials who similarly
adopted Egyptian cultural traits are also
attested: some may have been educated in
the Egyptian court, which tried to control
the conquered Nubian territory by securing
the allegiance of the Nubian elite, in part
through a policy of acculturation.

21 Signet-ring

Sai Island; New Kingdom, 18th Dynasty; SNM 31327; D 2.2 cm

A single piece of electrum (an alloy of gold and silver) was used to
fashion this ring, into which an ivory signet has been set. The signet
is decorated with an unusual design – a palm tree, topped with two
palm fronds, flanked on either side by a mirror. Interestingly, mirror
handles were frequently shaped like palm trunks. These mirrors would
have suggested not only the objects themselves, but could also have
been interpreted as the hieroglyphic sign for life (*ankh*), one of the
most common protective symbols. Signet rings of this type are rare
and were reserved for the elite.

23 Statue of Amenhotep II

Kumma; New Kingdom, 18th Dynasty
(1427–1400 BC); SNM 30; H 36.9 cm

Kneeling on a pedestal offering two pots,
probably of wine, the king wears royal
regalia including a kilt and striped
head-cloth (*nemes*) with a cobra (*uraeus*)
adorning his brow. Although this serene
figure lacks an inscription, he can be
identified stylistically as Pharaoh
Amenhotep II. This is also consistent with
the place where the statue was found.
An extensive building programme was
carried out by the Egyptian pharaohs of
the mid-18th Dynasty throughout Nubia,
strengthening their presence. The Kumma
temple was renovated and enlarged by
Amenhotep II, and this quartzite statue
seems to have been one of several of this
king placed there.

24 Foundation deposits of Thutmose IV

Dokki Gel; New Kingdom (1400–1390 BC); SNM 31203; jars: H 5.3–6.6 cm,
dishes: H 3.5–3.7 cm

Two deposits of ritual items were discovered, buried 0.5 m beneath
the sanctuary foundations of the New Kingdom temples at Dokki Gel.
Twenty-eight faience plaques, most bearing the names and epithets
of Thutmose IV, were recovered. These were found together with over
fifty miniature ceramic vessels, largely comprising dishes and jars,
a miniature model copper-alloy adze, and numerous tubular beads.
Foundation deposits such as these were magical offerings thought
to ensure the preservation of a building.

25 Stela of Amenhotep III

Sedeinga; New Kingdom, 18th Dynasty (1390–1352 BC); SNM 31216; preserved H 49 cm

Although this fragmentary sandstone stela was re-used in a Kushite tomb, it probably came from the temple of Queen Tiye, the Great Royal Wife of Amenhotep III, at Sedeinga. The stela shows Pharaoh Amenhotep III on the left, offering incense to the god Amun of Soleb and to his own deified likeness on the right. The ram's horn, wrapped around the deified king's ear, emphasizes his connections with the ram god Amun and draws attention to the relationship between the temples of Sedeinga and Soleb, located just a few kilometres to the south. Amun and some associated hieroglyphs were erased for religiously motivated reasons during the Amarna period (1352–1336 BC) and later re-carved possibly as early as the reign of Tutankhamun (1336–1327 BC).

26 Temple at Sedeinga

Founded at Sedeinga during the mid-18th Dynasty, this sandstone temple with elaborately carved Hathor-headed column capitals was probably dedicated to the cult of Queen Tiye, the Great Royal Wife of Amenhotep III (1390–1352 BC). Sedeinga was a major town during the Egyptian New Kingdom and formed part of an important Egyptian building programme between the Second and Third Cataracts of the Nile. It remained significant during the following Kushite period, when the temple was renovated by King Taharqo (690–664 BC). Two large cemeteries with numerous pyramids and funerary chapels (cats 46, 48) are associated with the Kushite settlement.

27 Stela of Seti I

Amara West; New Kingdom, 19th Dynasty (1294–1279 BC);
SNM 3063; H 59.7 cm

Seti I is shown here in fine relief with a scimitar
or *khepesh* sword, an emblem of divine strength,
smiting Nubian prisoners. The god Amen-Ra, no
longer preserved, presents a similar sword to the king.
Discovered in a temple built by Ramesses II, son of
Seti I, this sandstone stela probably commemorates
Seti's victory over the land of Irem in year eight of
his reign. Irem's locale is uncertain, but may have
incorporated the area south of the Fifth Cataract
of the Nile, a region within reach of punitive
expeditions, but too remote to be permanently
subjugated by the Egyptians.

28 Scimitar

Ez-Zuma; New Kingdom, possibly Ramesside; SNM 31316; L 58.8 cm

This copper-alloy scimitar, described by the ancient
Egyptians as a *khepesh* or 'foreleg of an ox' after its shape,
is the first to be discovered in Sudan. It was cast in one piece
and consists of a handle, from which the inlay is now
missing, a straight hilt and a convex cutting edge. Notches
in the blade indicate wear and regular use. The classical form
of *khepesh* has a profoundly curved blade and squared end
as is shown on the stela of Seti I (see cat. 27). This particular
variation may have been created for regular military use.

29 Beads

Hillat el-Arab; New Kingdom/Kushite (Napatan); SNM 31167, 31169, 31170 and 31171

This diverse assortment of ostrich eggshell, cowrie shell, carnelian and faience beads was discovered in the disturbed fill of a tomb, and certainly formed part of the original grave goods. In their rush to rob the tomb, the ancient thieves appear to have scattered these beads. Some were from gold and carnelian bead necklaces, while others, particularly the ostrich eggshell and faience discs, came from necklaces that contained many strings of amulets and beads. Not all material was acquired or manufactured locally: the cowrie shells were brought from the Red Sea. Beads are difficult to date as the types and styles evolved very slowly.

30 Cylinder of Aspelta

Nuri; Kushite (Napatan, 593–568 BC); SNM 1372;
H 7.5 cm

Nine of the royal tombs at Nuri contained
gold cylinders, and fifteen were found in the
tomb of King Aspelta alone. These sheaths
were constructed in three pieces: an upper
cylinder, a lower cylinder and an internal
liner, often of silver, onto which the other
two pieces were fitted. The goddess Hathor,
wearing a shift dress, is incised on the
cylinder exterior. She is flanked on either
side by the names of Aspelta. The use of
these objects is uncertain. The silver sleeve
within the cylinder contains wood
impressions, suggesting that these sheaths
may have capped the ends of wooden
sceptres, rods or sticks.

31 Amulet of a child

Sai Island; Kushite (Napatan); SNM 28770; H 6.8 cm

During the Late Period (747–330 BC), amulets were very popular
in Egypt and Nubia. This glazed amulet is of the naked child-god
Horus or Harpocrates, shown wearing a side-lock of hair, an
indicator of youth, with his arms at his sides. Often his finger is
placed at his mouth and he is depicted sitting on his mother's lap.
'Horus-the-Child' was believed to have the power to overcome
evil because he first escaped, then later defeated his father's
murderer, after being secreted in the Nile Delta by Isis, his
mother. Consequently, his amulets were thought to have great
protective powers.

32 The sacred mountain of Jebel Barkal

Downstream from the Fourth Cataract a large, flat-topped sandstone mountain, with a pinnacle protruding at one end, rises above the surrounding plain. Recognized as the sacred dwelling of the god Amun by both Egyptians and Nubians, it served as an important Kushite religious cult centre, rising to prominence during the eighth century BC and remaining so until the fourth century AD. The mountain shape was thought to symbolize the Kushite crown with the pinnacle at the front representing the cobra (*uraeus*) signifying kingship. Numerous large temples, including the Great Temple of Amun, and palaces were constructed at its base.

33 Statue of Anlamani

Jebel Barkal; Kushite (Napatan, 623–593 BC); SNM 1845;
H 2.15 m

Found among a cache of royal statue fragments, this granitic gneiss figure of the Kushite king Anlamani is roughly lifesize. While his skin was highly polished, his kilt, necklace, sandals and crown were left rough so that gilding could be applied. A hieroglyphic text bearing his name and titles runs down the sculpture's back pillar. Nine other lifesize or colossal royal statues were also deliberately smashed and buried just outside the Great Temple of Amun. It is thought that most had stood in a court in the Amun temple and were desecrated during an assault by the army of the Egyptian Pharaoh Psammtik II, who burned the temples and royal palace at Barkal in 593 BC.

34 Statue of Beset

Kawa; Kushite (Napatan); SNM 31116; H 1.03 m

This rare depiction of the naked goddess Beset displays many features commonly associated with the better known dwarf god Bes, including the crown of feathers on her head. Like Bes, it may have been believed that she was capable of warding off serpents as she grips a snake in either hand, their sinuous red bodies extending up her arms. Originally, this large ceramic Beset was set into the wall of a small temple, accompanied by a similar Bes figure. She is regarded as both his consort and mother, and is sometimes shown suckling him. Bes and Beset were seen as protective deities connected with sexuality, the family, women and childbirth.

35 Bottle

Kerma; Kushite (Napatan);
SNM 31206; H 17.5 cm

Skilfully manufactured, the stylish lines of this delicate little egg-shaped faience bottle are accentuated by the ribbed decoration. It was found *in situ* in a woman's tomb. She lay in a crouched position with her arm bent near her face; the bottle had been put in her hand and rested against her brow. An Egyptian faience flask had also been placed near her head.

36 Sphinx of Senkamanisken

Jebel Barkal; Kushite (Napatan, 643–623 BC); SNM 1852;
H 88.3 cm

Senkamanisken is depicted as a powerful sphinx,
a lion with a bearded human head, wearing the
royal striped head-cloth (*nemes*) and a double
crown. Upon his forehead are two *uraei*, or cobras,
symbols of Kushite kingship. The sphinx has
human hands and arms, instead of lion's paws,
which is rather unusual. He proffers an offering
jar inscribed with the king's names.

This granite statue was found just inside the
entry to the Great Amun Temple at Barkal, along
with many fragments of other figures, suggesting
that the temple had once been filled with statues
of Egyptian and Kushite rulers and dignitaries.

37 Statue of Amun

Jebel Barkal; Kushite (Meroitic, third–first
centuries BC); SNM 1844; H 60 cm

Amun, the god who resides in Jebel Barkal,
is shown with a ram's head and a man's
body. He wears a royal kilt (*shendyt*) and has
a socket on his head which probably once
held a gilded crown of two large, upright
feathers and a sun disc with cobra (*uraeus*).
Discovered buried beneath huge rocks, near
a granite altar in the sanctuary of a small
temple to Amun, this granite statue may
have been the temple's sacred cult image.
This temple had been built at the foot of
the mountain, so close, in fact, that it was
repeatedly damaged by rockfalls.

38 Statuette of a Kushite king

Tabo; Kushite (Meroitic); SNM 24705; H 50 cm

This is the largest copper-alloy statue discovered in Sudan and thus far has no parallels. Gold, applied over plaster, still remains on parts of the face and chest. The figure of this unidentified king has a narrow waist, broad shoulders and is striding forward purposefully. His arms are bent to suggest motion. He wears a kilt, sandals, armlets and a pectoral necklace with three ram-headed amulets. A cap of tight curls, with streamers or ribbons down the back and a circlet with two cobras (*uraei*) on the front, signifies kingship. An archer's thumb-ring is visible on the right hand and it has been suggested that this statue portrays the king as an archer, perhaps symbolizing his military leadership.

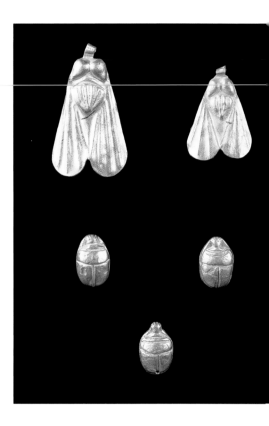

39 Flies and scarabs

Wadi Terfowi; late second–early first centuries BC; SNM 31347 and
31353; flies: L 2.7 and 3.7 cm; scarabs: L 1.6 cm

Seventeen gold ornaments were found wrapped in a cloth
and hidden in a robbed tomb where they may have
formed part of a thief's stash. Among them were these
scarab and fly amulets. Both flies have suspension loops
and could be worn as pendants. In Egypt, during the New
Kingdom, flies were believed to have the power to avert
evil and were frequently awarded as military decorations
for bravery, and perhaps persistence. Scarabs, connected
with the scarab sun-god Khepri, were associated with
resurrection. It is not known what meaning the Kushites
attributed to these insects.

40 The city of Naga

Isolated in the desert margins east of the Nile Valley
lie the remains of the Kushite city of Naga. It is known
for its spectacular, monumental religious buildings,
particularly the Lion Temple of the Kushite god
Apedemak, the Temple of Amun and the so-called
'Roman Kiosk'. These monuments, particularly the
latter, display a mixture of Egyptian, Graeco-Roman
and local artistic and architectural styles. With two
man-made water reservoirs (*hafir*) providing
valuable water supplies during the dry season, the
royal city of Naga embodied the authority and
power of the Kushite state over the nomadic and
semi-nomadic population residing on the desert edge.

41 Statue of Natakamani

Naga; Kushite (Meroitic, first century AD);
SNM 30115b; H 38 cm

Holding a crook, flail and sceptre, capped
with the hieroglyphic sign for life (*ankh*),
Natakamani is shown mummy-shaped,
wearing a royal beard and striped head-cloth
(*nemes*). He is represented as a royal version
of Amun's son, the god Khonsu, with the
head-cloth replacing Khonsu's usual side-
lock of hair. This sandstone statue originally
stood between the forelegs of one of the
twelve rams lining the avenue leading up to
the Temple of Amun (see cat. 40). As such,
the king was symbolically shown as the son
of Amun and was protected by the ram form
of his father, the god.

42 Bark stand

Naga; Kushite (Meroitic, first century AD);
SNM 31331; H 1.323 m

Miraculously undamaged, this sandstone
altar was discovered in its original position in
the sanctuary of the Amun temple. All four
sides are decorated with well-cut relief that
visually creates a three-dimensional effect.
On the front, the falcon-headed Horus and
ibis-headed Thoth fasten papyrus around the
hieroglyphic windpipe sign (*sma*). The names
of the rulers, King Natakamani and Queen
Amanitore, are carved in between them in
Meroitic hieroglyphs. In Egypt, the binding of
the *sma* symbolized the unification of Upper
and Lower Egypt. This motif was adopted
and modified by the Kushites to represent
order and political and cosmic stability
under Kushite rule.

43 Stela of Amanishakheto and the goddess Amesemi

Naga; Kushite (Meroitic, first century BC); SNM 31338; H 25.5 cm

Queen Amanishakheto and the goddess Amesemi are carved in high-quality relief and identified by Meroitic hieroglyphs. Both wear close-fitting shift dresses, curled caps and fringed scarves, but physically are shown in different ways. Amesemi is slim, has facial scars and wears a finely decorated dress and complex crown. Amanishakheto, an extremely heavy woman, is dressed simply and wears a plain circlet around her head. While the queen raises her arm worshipping Amesemi, the goddess gives her the gift of divine breath. This is shown as a chain of small life signs (*ankh*) running from the nose of the goddess to that of the queen. A Meroitic religious hymn is inscribed on the back and sides of the sandstone stela: its meaning remains elusive as the Meroitic language has yet to be deciphered.

44 Vase with frogs

Sedeinga; Kushite (Meroitic); SNM 27368; H 33 cm

The black-painted decoration on this ceramic vase, with a series of four rather grumpy-looking frogs, is striking against the light brown. Between each frog the symbol of life (*ankh*) blooms from a stem. In Egypt and the Graeco-Roman world the frog symbolized creation, fertility and eternal life, perhaps in part because frogs appeared to be born directly from the Nile mud. Globular bottles with long necks have often been found in tombs at the entry to the burial chamber. It is likely that they were used during the funeral ritual, in which a meal was shared with the deceased before the tomb was sealed.

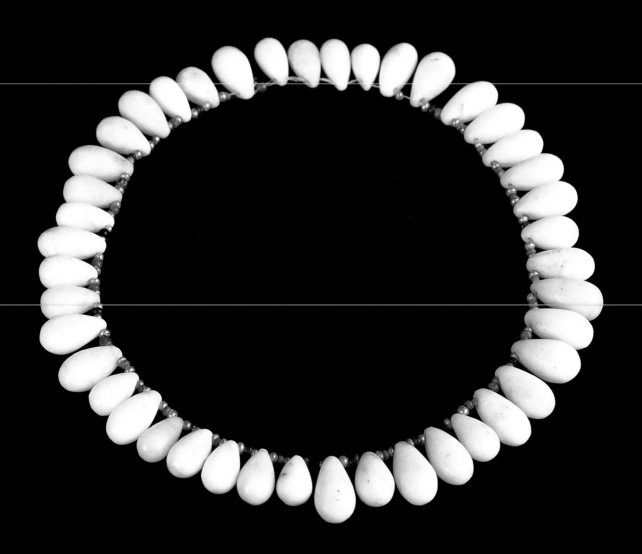

45 Necklace

Sai Island; Kushite (Meroitic); SNM 28779; L 50 cm

Tiny carnelian or glass beads separate the milky white quartz pendants of this necklace, which was discovered by the excavator strung precisely in this fashion. This type of teardrop-shaped bead was common during the late Kushite period and is found widely distributed.

46 Door jamb with the image of Anubis

Sedeinga; Kushite (Meroitic, second century AD); SNM 23060; H 88 cm

Netemkhor, a man of note in the second century AD, built his tomb beneath a pyramid at Sedeinga. A funerary chapel was erected on the east side of the pyramid, strategically blocking the entry to the underground tomb chamber. The chapel's sandstone door jambs were decorated with images of gods. Here Anubis, richly adorned with numerous armlets and anklets, pours an offering of water from a breast-shaped vessel (*situla*) in honour of Netemkhor. A goddess, engaged in the same activity, would have been depicted on the opposing jamb. These chapels were often so small that it would have been impossible to conduct any ceremonies inside them.

47 Pyramids at Meroe

Steeper and smaller than their Egyptian
counterparts to the north, Kushite pyramids
also contained no rooms, but were solid
structures built over the top of underground
burial chambers. In many instances the
burial chambers were filled and sealed
before the pyramid was even constructed.
Built from the eighth century BC to fourth
century AD, there are nearly 300 pyramids
in Sudan, and it was the funerary monument
favoured by the Kushite royal family, nobles
and wealthy individuals. The pyramids
shown here, from the south cemetery at
Meroe, were constructed for members of
the royal family residing there.

48 Head of a *ba*-statue

Sedeinga; Kushite (Meroitic, second–third centuries AD); SNM 31118; H 15.7 cm

In the afterlife, a person's spirit or personality was believed to take
the form of a human-headed bird (*ba*) that could fly between the
body of the deceased and the underworld. *Ba*-statues were frequently
associated with tombs, probably to assist in reuniting the body with
its *ba*. This outstanding head of a sandstone *ba*-statue, carved in the
distinctive Kushite style, shows a serene man with wide eyes, tight
curls, a dimpled chin and a handsome smile. A hole in the top of the
head may have once held a golden disc, and traces of ochre indicate
the statue had been painted.

49 Jar

Gabati; Kushite (Meroitic, first century AD); SNM 27818;
H 13.3 cm

Few elaborate faience vessels have been found in
Sudan and, unlike this sophisticated jar, most are
undecorated. The pattern circling this one may have
been derived from a combination of the *sa* knot,
symbolizing protection, and the *djed* pillar,
representing stability. Ornate faience vessels have
been found in Egypt, and it is possible that this
jar was made by an Egyptian workshop and
subsequently imported.

50 Bell from the trappings of a horse

El-Hobagi; Post-Meroitic, fourth–fifth centuries AD;
SNM 26302; H 10.8 cm

Decorated with two rows of guinea-fowl, this
copper-alloy bell was provided with a suspension
ring that would have allowed it to dangle from
the tack of a horse, chiming when the animal
moved. Unearthed in a funeral mound, it was
accompanied by other horse trappings and
fragments of cattle skulls. The presence of these
objects could suggest that animals were sacrificed
as part of the funerary rites. Horses and their tack
were often included in late Kushite royal burials;
the discovery of this bell in a Post-Meroitic tomb
may suggest that this custom continued later.

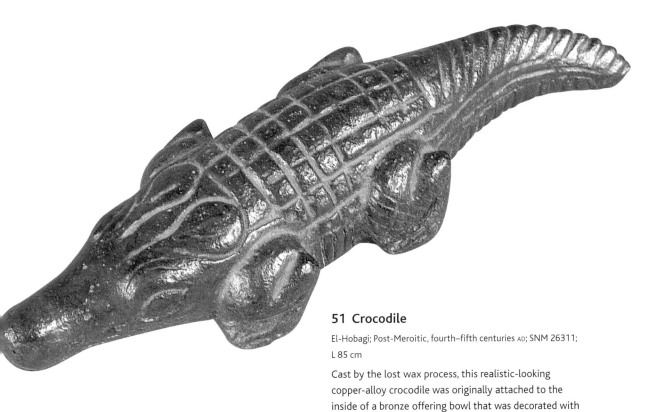

51 Crocodile

El-Hobagi; Post-Meroitic, fourth–fifth centuries AD; SNM 26311; L 85 cm

Cast by the lost wax process, this realistic-looking copper-alloy crocodile was originally attached to the inside of a bronze offering bowl that was decorated with falcons and flowers. When the bowl was filled, the crocodile would be submerged. It would gradually reappear as the liquid was poured out. As this effect was probably deliberate, it may have been of special significance in the rituals in which the bowl was used.

52 Wall painting

Faras; medieval, twelfth century AD;
SNM 24362; Virgin Mary figure:
H 1.75 m

The Virgin Mary, carrying the
infant Jesus on her left arm,
embraces the smaller figure of a
Nubian queen in a gesture of
protection. Both the Virgin and
Child are bending their heads
slightly towards the queen, making
the spiritual contact among all
three individuals clearly visible.
The little cross on the queen's
forehead proclaims her faith.
She is richly dressed in full court
splendour, signifying that she is
without doubt a person of high
rank. The painting is a classic
votive image, painted in a church
to obtain grace and salvation for a
given individual. The purse in the
queen's hand clearly shows that
she is the patron or benefactor.

53 Column capitals at Old Dongola

Old Dongola was the capital of the medieval kingdom of Makuria. Initially it was a heavily fortified citadel built along the banks of the Nile in the fifth century AD; after Christianity was adopted as the state religion during the sixth century AD, a bishopric was established here. The city expanded, and numerous large elaborate churches, cathedrals, monasteries, palaces and a vast housing district were built. Nubian artistic expression flowered, and painting, basketry, metalworking, textile and pottery production all reached high technological standards. Christian symbols were frequently incorporated into decorations, and are most commonly found on pottery, but they also appear on column capitals, in paintings and even window grills.

54 Pottery stamp

Old Dongola; medieval; SNM 31213; H 6 cm

Although the animal incised on this ceramic stamp resembles a
gazelle, it is identified as the Lamb of God by the Greek inscription
that accompanies it. The Holy Lamb stands before a chalice and a loaf
of eucharistic bread. The stamp could have been used to decorate
pottery and has a convenient hole on the upper part through which
a string or leather strap could be threaded, allowing the stamp to
be hung or worn. Many small medieval bowls are embellished with
stamped centrepieces. However, this ceramic stamp, which was found
in a monastery, may also have been used to decorate eucharistic
bread loaves prior to baking.

55 Chalice

Khalil el-Kubra; medieval, sixth–eighth centuries AD;
SNM 26941; H 31 cm

Uncovered by a farmer digging for fertile agricultural
soil, this ceramic chalice is one of the few complete
Soba Ware vessels discovered to date. Named after
the site where it was first found and probably
manufactured, the colour, diamond patterns and
repeating white, cross-shaped decoration are typical
of Soba Ware. Strangely enough, the chalice seems
to have come from a grave, which is probably why it
remained so well preserved. Soba Ware is usually
found in fragments scattered over the sites of ancient
towns. Since Christian burials normally lack grave
goods, it is possible that a pagan was buried with this
vessel, a type characteristic of the Early Christian
period in the medieval kingdom of Alwa.

56 Starburst lamp

Old Dongola; medieval; SNM 31358; H 4 cm

Forming a thirteen-petal rosette, this schist lamp shows signs of intensive use. It was found among the rubble within a monastery and extracted from within a solid mass of burnt oil. When in use, a wick would have been placed in each of the rosette's petals. The wick ends were soaked in oil stored in the round depression in the centre of the lamp. Probably imported, this object is so far unique in Nubia. Similar objects have been found as far away as Iraq.

57 Funerary stela

Badi'; Islamic, AD 1015; SNM 24379; H 43 cm

Written in Kufi Arabic, this is the felsite funerary stela of Mohamed ibn Mahmoud ibn Ahmed ibn al-Walid, who died in AH 405 (AD 1015) during the eighth month (*Sha'ban*) of the Islamic calendar. Although the beginning of the inscription is missing, four Koranic verses from sura 112 (sura Ikhlas) are preserved. Islamization was a gradual process in Sudan and the presence of this early Arabic tombstone attests to the spread of Muslims into the country. Beginning during the seventh century AD, Muslims co-existed with Christians until the end of the medieval kingdom of Makuria (c. AD 1365), when Christianity began to decline.

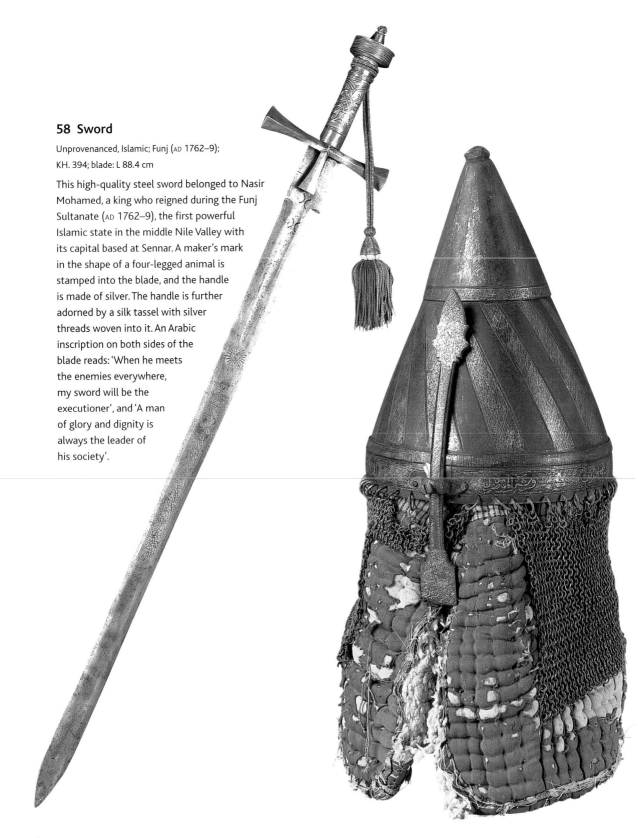

58 Sword

Unprovenanced, Islamic; Funj (AD 1762–9);
KH. 394; blade: L 88.4 cm

This high-quality steel sword belonged to Nasir
Mohamed, a king who reigned during the Funj
Sultanate (AD 1762–9), the first powerful
Islamic state in the middle Nile Valley with
its capital based at Sennar. A maker's mark
in the shape of a four-legged animal is
stamped into the blade, and the handle
is made of silver. The handle is further
adorned by a silk tassel with silver
threads woven into it. An Arabic
inscription on both sides of the
blade reads: 'When he meets
the enemies everywhere,
my sword will be the
executioner', and 'A man
of glory and dignity is
always the leader of
his society'.

59 Helmet

Unprovenanced, Islamic; Turkiya (AD 1820–81), reused during the
Mahdiya (AD 1881–98); KH. 409; helmet: max. H with silk padding
55 cm

Used over a long period of time, this cone-shaped iron
helmet is adorned with a chainmail curtain around the rim
and lined with soft padding to protect the neck when
worn. Originally the helmet was painted black then gilded
with gold leaf: bands of gilding spiral up the helmet. Arabic
writing inscribed on the gilding around the rim reads:
'In the name of Allah, the compassionate, the merciful,
I will follow the will of the God as he will bestow upon
you other blessings which you desire, help from Allah and
speedy victory. Proclaim the good tidings to the faithful'.

60 Qubba Sheikh Idriss

Islamic holy men, or Sheikhs, and saints
were often buried under these substantial
superstructures known as *qubba*. Most are
shaped like domes and whitewashed;
however, the shape of this particular tomb,
Qubba Sheikh Idriss, located at Koyekka,
evokes the pyramids of the earlier Kushite
period. Found scattered throughout northern
Sudan, *qubba* are visible monuments of a
living Islamic faith.

Recommended reading

Adams, W.Y. 1982. *Nubia Corridor to Africa*. 2nd edn. London.

Davies, V. and R. Friedman 1998. *Egypt*. London.

Morkot, R. 2000. *The Black Pharaohs*. London.

O'Connor, D. and S. Quirke (eds) 2003. *Mysterious Lands*. London.

O'Connor, D. and A. Reid (eds) 2003. *Ancient Egypt in Africa*. London.

Shinnie, P.L. 1996. *Ancient Nubia*. London.

Smith, S.T. 2003. *Wretched Kush. Ethnic Identities in Egypt's Nubian Empire*. London–New York.

Taylor, J.H. 1991. *Egypt and Nubia*. London.

Welsby, D.A. 1996. *The Kingdom of Kush*. London.

Welsby, D.A. 2002. *The Medieval Kingdoms of Nubia*. London.

Welsby, D.A. and J.R. Anderson (eds) 2004. *Sudan: Ancient Treasures*. London.

Acknowledgements

The British Museum and its Department of Ancient Egypt and Sudan gratefully acknowledge the support of the many people, too numerous to name individually here, museums, institutions and authorities who contributed to the creation of the exhibition *Sudan: Ancient Treasures* and to the accompanying publications including the present volume. Special thanks are due to:

HE Abdel Jaleel Al-Basha, Minister of Tourism and National Heritage, Sudan
HE Hasan Abdin, Sudanese Ambassador to the United Kingdom
The Embassy of the Republic of the Sudan in London
HE William Patey, British Ambassador to the Sudan
The British Embassy to the Sudan in Khartoum
Hassan Hussein Idris Ahmed, Director General, National Corporation
    for Antiquities and Museums, Sudan
Colleagues from the National Corporation for Antiquities and Museums, Sudan
Colleagues from the University of Khartoum and University of Dongola
The many colleagues who supported and collaborated with us,
    and who contributed text and photographs to the catalogues and exhibition
Colleagues from other departments in the British Museum,
    and Laura Brockbank and staff of the British Museum Press, London
Rocco Ricci
Francoise Morasso
Harry Green
Johanna Stephenson
Kaliopee Fiske
The Pagoulatos family and staff of the Acropole Hotel, Khartoum
Fundación 'la Caixa', Madrid
The Sudan Archaeological Research Society

Translations
Abdel Rahman Ali Mohamed
Okasha El Daly
Fathi Khider
Caroline Rocheleau
Isabella Welsby Sjöström

Photographic acknowledgements
Page 6: D.A. Welsby
Page 8: Map by Claire Thorne © The British Museum
Page 9: Chronology by Harry Green © The British Museum

All catalogue photography by Rocco Ricci © The British Museum,
apart from the following catalogue entries:
2–3 Philippa Pearce
5, 6, 8, 9, 10, 12, 16, 19, 22, 27, 36, 37, 38, 44, 46,
    50, 51, 57 Rocco Ricci © The Sudan National Museum
7 ACACIA project, University of Cologne
13 D. Berti, courtesy of the Mission archéologique
    de l'Université de Genève à Kerma au Soudan
26, 32, 40, 47, 53, 60 D.A. Welsby